7 Simple Tricks to Remembering Names

How to Recall Names of People You Meet

TRAVIS TYLER

Legal & Disclaimer

The information contained in this book and its contents is not designed to replace or take the place of any form of medical or professional advice and is not meant to replace the need for independent medical, financial, legal, or other professional advice or services as may be required. The contents and information in this book have been provided for educational and entertainment purposes only.

The contents and information contained in this book have been compiled from sources deemed reliable, and it is accurate to the best of the Author's knowledge, information, and belief. However, the Author cannot guarantee its accuracy and validity and cannot be held liable for any errors and/or omissions. Further, changes are periodically made to this book as and when needed. Where appropriate and/or necessary, you must consult a professional (including but not limited to your doctor, attorney, financial advisor, or such other professional advisor) before using any of the suggested remedies, techniques, or information in this book.

Upon using the contents and information contained in this book, you agree to hold harmless the Author from and against any damages, costs, and expenses, including any legal fees potentially resulting from the application of any of the information provided by this book. This disclaimer applies to any loss, damages, or injury caused by the use and application, whether directly or indirectly, of any advice or information presented, whether for breach of contract, tort, negligence, personal injury, criminal intent, or under any other cause of action.

You agree to accept all risks of using the information presented inside this book.

By continuing to read this book you agree that, where appropriate and/or necessary, you shall consult a professional (including but not limited to your doctor, attorney, or financial advisor or such other advisor as needed) before using any of the suggested remedies, techniques, or information in this book.

TABLE OF CONTENTS

INTRODUCTION

Why is it so easy to forget someone's name?

We've all been there. You're introduced to someone and immediately wonder what the heck their name is. And it can be horrible—the cold, creeping sense of shame and dread that twists at your stomach. You hope beyond all hope that you won't need to use their name because you honestly have no idea what it is. There's possibly nothing more embarrassing in a social situation. But, you can take solace: this phenomenon is very, common, and there's even a scientific condition related to it. While few of us can say we suffer from prosopagnosia—the physical inability to recognize people we've met or know—most of us have indeed committed the faux pas of forgetting a name.

It's all because our brains are really clever in the way they actively make decisions without us even knowing about it. Your subconscious mind will weigh risk and reward, continually calculate, sort important from unimportant information, and react accordingly. It can decide whether you step in a puddle or go around it, whether you instinctively catch something or shield your face from it, or whether to remember or forget the snippets of conversation you hear in the street. The same goes for meeting people. Your brain decides, without your realizing, whether or not this is an important person and either remembers their name or doesn't. But focusing your mind on the task at hand and consciously deciding that this person's name is important information, well, that'll go a long way toward helping you remember names before we even get into the methodologies below.

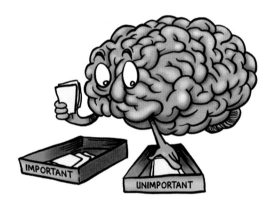

So, let's get to it—seven tricks and tips that will help you memorize the names of even the most forgettable people—and save you some embarrassment in the process too.

CHAPTER 1:

REPETITION

How repeating someone's name can help it stick

We've all heard it. It's the oldest trick in the book. Repeating someone's name can help you remember it. While it is an old adage, the saying is also true. Repetition is one of the most common forms of memory retention (and one of the most effective too). That's why the technique is used in schools to teach children, in the military to train troops, in farmyards to teach dogs, and on sports fields to win matches. Exploiting the "practice makes perfect" notion is the same thing.

Memory doesn't pertain only to figures or data. It also has to do with things like remembering the words to your favorite song. Some people who cannot remember where they left their keys or the items on their groceries list, can recall entire songs from their childhood. Muscle memory, like the ability to kick a perfect field goal, or image recall, like remembering faces—are just different aspects of the same concept. A concert pianist may be talented, but it takes a lot of practice and a lot of repetition to play like that. Their minds can recall the memory of the last thousand times they did it and apply that knowledge in real time. You may think it's your fingers, your foot, or your mouth (when it comes to karaoke), but it's not—it's your brain.

Repeating things to yourself over long, or short, periods will help them stick, and that's a fact. Now, most of us are really well practiced at this anyway. Mothers are likely to be great at remembering everything their kids have to do in the coming week, accountants have an excellent memory for numbers, and a mechanic knows exactly what goes back where when they're rebuilding an engine. It's a process that is honed over time. However, as well as these long-term repetitions, we also have a lot of short-term repetitions going on that help us remember things we've just learned.

Repetition is something we all do without thinking; it's the fastest way to embed something into your memory. If someone asks you to remember a phone number while they type it in, you'll repeat it continually in your head to keep it in mind. The same goes if you're trying to remember a shopping list. But, there is another side to it beyond the simple "keeping it in mind."

Repetition is an effective memory tool, and the reason is quite basic. We remember things thanks to a process called assimilation. Every time we are introduced to something new, our brain automatically tries to connect that new piece of information with something we already know. It's the fundamental idea that for our brains to store something effectively, we need to understand it intrinsically. We do this by assimilating new information into existing information and lumping together similar ideas and data so we can categorize them. When we do this, we create new neural links between new pieces of information and old ones. The more a pathway is traveled, the more embedded and permanent it becomes. This is a great visual tool for imagining how repetition works. In your brain, you have a central idea, like the name of your new coworker. Surrounding that, you have the names of everyone you know. Your parents, your siblings, your best friends, your spouse, or partner—they are names you think about and use a lot. By doing that, you're constantly wearing that pathway in, making it more and more permanent. It's like walking through a field. If you walk the same path every day, eventually, that grass will never grow back, no matter how long it's left unwalked. But, if you walk a path once and then leave it, the grass will spring back up soon after, and the pathway will disappear.

This is how assimilation works. Your brain is always scanning for chunks of information without well-trodden pathways, and if it finds something floating absently, it'll get rid of it. You can make use of this idea. When you meet someone for the first time, immediately repeat their name in your head several times. Then, when you ask a question, use their name again. And then again. And when you bid them adieu, use it again. "It was great to meet you, David," or whatever their name is. While this may seem a little heavy handed or like it will make you look strange, it will in fact help. And the next time, you'll remember their name.

While this is the most effective and easiest way to establish a pathway, there is a less-outward method which, when practiced, will serve you just as well. While repeating someone's name out loud at a party or in a bar may be perfectly acceptable, doing it on a date or, heaven forbid, in a new business venture, can make you look a little silly. A potential personal or business partner will no doubt spot your explicit repetition and notice that you're trying to remember their name. This will make them feel unmemorable and will likely result in an unfavorable outcome. No one wants to be forgotten. However, don't despair; thinking a name works too. When you ask someone, "Where are you from?" adding "David" in your head as though you were saying it out loud will help to establish those pathways. While you're talking to David, repeating his name in natural speech patterns, even in thought, will help you remember. Simply saying "David" over and over in your head will have less of an effect. Your brain will always try to make sense of things, so giving a name context and allowing it to assimilate, be it in thought or speech, will help you remember it.

CHAPTER 2:

IMAGE LINKING

Because a picture is worth a thousand names

Image linking is just what it sounds like: connecting an image to—well—anything. It relies on the brain's ability for image recall rather than its data recall. Recalling data that has no physical form (like a name) can be tough. Our minds try to sift through trillions of bytes of data, searching for it. Often, we will get close but won't be able to remember it. You've probably been there, running into someone you met a while back. He says hello, and you do too. He asks about the kids, and you tell him they're good. You ask about his, and while he's rambling, you're thinking, "Damn, what's this guy's name? Is it Steve? Stan? No, that's not right…Sam? Simon?" You know it's something beginning with "S," but in the tumult of your mind, the field is too wide, and now suddenly, your brain is telling you his name is "Sausage." You've got images of sausages flying through your head, and you don't know why.

The human brain is great at image recall. Don't believe me? Picture the face of your mother or your father. Easy? Picture your first car or a childhood pet. Still easy? What about Mona Lisa? A billboard you pass on the way to work? What about the Eiffel Tower? The way Earth looks from space? You may not have seen them other than in a photo. But those images can be as strong in your mind as a loved one's face. By exploiting this trait while playing on your brain's ability to make connections (remember Simon and Sausage), you can assign images to people you meet based on a link they have. You can then use that already well-trodden neural pathway to get to the right name. It sounds complicated, but considering your brain's computing power, it's really not.

Basic Image Linking

If you meet someone named Donald, you may assign him as Donald Duck in your mind. You can use whatever you'd like, but often it's best to go with your instincts. Upon being introduced to Simon, if that is his name, you may well think "Ah, like Simon Cowell." Whether you say it or not is irrelevant. But if you focus on that image, you can form a link between this new person and Simon Cowell. If you do, you'll begin to make more connections—the love of sweaters, the bad haircut, the overly white teeth. Maybe he has all of them; maybe he has none. The point is, you're attributing a new set of data to an existing set. Your brain recalls existing data with ease because it's already earmarked as important information. Linking the new person's face to existing data gives it more importance and ensures your brain doesn't discard it. You'll likely remember Simon Cowell's face when you see new Simon's face, and that's fine because you have his name.

This isn't a permanent link, because after you meet Simon a few times, you'll get to know him. The repetition of that will embed in your memory, and in the future, you could break the news that the initial way you remembered his name was by comparing him to Simon Cowell. Who knows? He may even find it funny.

The link may be a simple one, like Donald to Donald Duck, or something utterly obscure, like remembering someone's name is Sue because when you met her, you immediately thought, "Oh, like Tiramisu. What a great dessert." As long as you have a strong picture of that delicious Italian confection in mind, you can assign that image to her, and when you see her again, your brain will recognize that you know her and pull up a picture of tiramisu. You've got your answer.

Mnemonic Image Linking

The other side of image linking is to employ a mnemonic device. We'll go deeper into mnemonics later, but for now, we'll look at their relevance to image linking. Often, we can recognize someone but can't remember their name. The brain has a knack for remembering faces. Dr. Doris Tsao, a neuroscientist and professor of biology at the California Institute of Technology, determined that the temporal lobe area of the brain contained six areas or "face patches" which became more active when looking at faces. A later study conducted by Le Chang, another neuroscientist, revealed that neurons responded based on just one dimension or feature of the face. To a neuron, a face is merely a group of different parts. By relying on our brain's knack for recognizing faces and our ability for image recall, as well as our natural love for rhyming, we can visually combine them in our minds. The basic premise is to immediately connect someone's name with a rhyming word and visualize them interacting. For example, if you meet a Mike, you could rhyme it with "bike." In your head, imagine Mike riding around on his bike, waving, falling off, or whatever is strong in your mind. Make it funny; our brains have a proclivity for remembering funny stuff. Next time you meet Mike, you'll likely think of a bike and leap to "Mike."

Of course, not everyone has a name that can easily be rhymed. An example of this may be a name like "Cassandra." Take a moment to think of something that rhymes. Can't do it? Not to worry. You can take specific sounds from the name and use them as triggers. "Cassandra" can become "Cas-Sand-Dra." So maybe you envisage Cassandra standing on the parapet of a castle on a sandy beach protected by a dragon. It might take a little effort, but even if something can't be rhymed, you can build on in this way. When you see the castle, the dragon, the beach, and Cassandra waving to you gleefully from the top of the wall, your mind will connect the dots and identify those triggers, and you will recall Cassandra's name. Now, the more complex these triggers are, the more practice they'll take, so don't take this method lightly; it needs dedication to master. However, despite this being easier for some names than others, it's a great method for remembering names and lets you exploit not only image recall but mnemonics too.

If, however, you were never good at rhymes and are drawing a blank, don't worry about it, because there is one more trick using visual triggers: the random-trigger technique.

Randomized Mnemonic Image Linking

This is most effective when you have a snap thought about someone you meet. Defining physical attributes or outward manifestations are likely to trigger the automatic subconscious connections your brain makes. If you meet someone with a physical attribute you find yourself drawn to (for example, if they're very tall, very short, overweight, or bald, or if they have strikingly blue eyes or scarily long fingernails), this is likely something that will stick with you. Or, regarding an outward manifestation, it may be someone's loud laugh, the way they clear their nose every few minutes, or their excessive nodding while listening. The brain is awesome at observing and cataloging these features of a person—much better than it is at remembering names—especially if you disapprove of them or are irked by them. Again, it is not advisable to say these things out loud, nor should you actively search for them. But if you find that your brain is drawing your attention to them, exploit that to help you remember the person's name: "Fat Bobby," "Fingernails Stacy," "Hilarious Steven," "Hannah Nods-a-Lot," "Tall Alex." You will automatically give this a subconscious rhythm, and it may well help you remember that person's name.

Mnemonic Image Linking and Remembering Multiple Names

As a final word on mnemonics, the technique presented above is the best tool to use when you are presented with a group of people whose names you need to remember.

Sitting at a table at a dinner party is a perfect example. You want the peas, but they are over there next to that guy in the red shirt. You met him in the kitchen, but what was his name again? If you only need a name for one night, you can latch onto something physical or outward: "Freddy Red-Shirt." And he's sitting next to "Davey Neck-Tie." To his left is "Sally Two-Chins," and on the end is "Bobby Cue-Ball." By finding something as a visual trigger and exaggerating these names, you can help yourself remember multiple names. And as a step further, why not imagine that this isn't just a dinner party, but the secret meeting of two mafia families. You've seen the movies where gangsters are called "Johnny Tight Lips" or "Fingers Malone." Why not put yourself in this world and see if it helps? We will go into more detail with this in our final trick later, but who knows? It could be the trick that saves you at the next Thanksgiving at the neighbor's house.

CHAPTER 3:

SPELL IT OUT

There's a blackboard in your head. No really, there is...

We are sticking with the image retention method for this one while combining it with another simple memory trick—writing it down. It is often easier to remember things after they have been written down. Simply listening can commit whatever it is we are dealing with to memory, but writing information down has a proven track record with recall. It is not so much the visual input of seeing things in writing as the physical act of writing that makes them stick. The focus that our brain exerts in converting mental to physical—in making our hands form the words or numbers we are trying to remember—helps the data to become ingrained.

I am sure all of us remember doing revisions in school and, more often, being made to write things down. When preparing for spelling tests, we were instructed to repeatedly write the words on our spelling list. If writing things down didn't help us to remember, why were we asked to do writing exercises at all? Why didn't our teachers simply ask us to remember instead? Writing didn't only give us something to refer to; it was the physical act that helped embed the information. The brain is a wonderfully clever thing. The information we absorb through our senses—sight, sound, smell, taste, and touch—is processed in separate sections of the brain. When we write something down, we have to focus our eyes (sight) on the page and use a lot of brainpower to coordinate our hands (touch). Forming each letter, one after another, keeping them straight on the page—that is a tall order. But, because the brain expends so much energy when we write, and more than one section of the brain is engaged, it registers that the information must be important. Remember how we talked about our brain sorting the useful from useless data input and getting rid of the stuff it didn't need? Well, this is the opposite. If we spend time and effort doing this, our brain is more likely to commit whatever we write down to memory. It is why handwriting is such a revered revision tactic; rewriting notes and transcripts by hand is something that a lot of teachers swear by.

We can go one step further with this and talk about the notion of muscle memory too. Once again, let's take a pianist for example. Though a pianist may be skilled at playing notes, learning a new piece takes time. By practicing and repeating, the brain becomes more comfortable with the movements and the piece in question. At some point, a pianist's mind can transcend their fingers. Many musicians find themselves twitching their fingers in time to music in their heads, practicing imaginary pianos, guitars, or flutes. In this way, a musician can keep a piece of music fresh in their memory for weeks without ever actually playing it. This goes to show the creation capacity of the human brain in relation to both sound and vision.

Using this capability and combining it with the known memory trick of writing things down, we can effectively create a chalkboard in our heads and visualize writing the person's name. While it works best to physically do it, you can't carry a pad and pen with you and write down everyone's name—that would look weird. What you can do, though, is imagine a big blackboard and visualize yourself writing a name as many times as you want. Keep that image clear in your head and keep writing it down. Every time you do, you strengthen that neural pathway. Give it a try; if it works for you, you will have another tool in your memory collection.

CHAPTER 4:

INFORMATION GROUPING

Who are you, where are you from, and what do you do?

Information grouping is also known as chunking. In psychology, chunking is defined as a collection of simpler and more familiar pieces of information that have been linked and stored in memory many times over. Then, when a single piece of information is required—like a name—the "chunk" acts as a group to help the name rise to the top.

To simplify information grouping or chunking, think of your brain as an utter mess of information that constantly swirls like a top-loading washer. Tossing a single sock into a full machine lets it get caught up in the tumult, and you lose it. It's the same with your brain. A single name going into the washing machine of your brain will likely never be found again. But a larger item, like a bedsheet, may be easier to spot and pick out.

We are still trying to accentuate natural processes that your brain follows, but by exaggerating and emphasizing them, we force our brains to become aware of themselves. This is the key to all memory tricks: knowing and visualizing how your brain stores information helps you retrieve it—you know where it is.

This knowledge has to do with another trick we will come to a little later, but in short, it's linked to information grouping. When you search for a song online, it's likely to be tagged in a variety of ways: by artist, by album, by genre, by similar songs, by popularity, by year of release; the list goes on. Of course, a lot of them overlap. You may have Taylor Swift and Led Zeppelin grouped together by popularity and Led Zeppelin and Grand Funk Railroad grouped by genre, but you'd be hard-pressed to find anywhere that Grand Funk Railroad and Taylor Swift are put together. It's the same thing in your head. You take on information like names and faces, and you group that information and store it, tagging it for later. You may well tag "Greg" as a name or even as the name of a male, but beyond that, you won't have much to go on. "Greg" suddenly gets filed away with all the other names, and when it comes time to retrieve it, you have nothing to pair it with. You see a nondescript man, and your brain presents you with a hundred names, any of which could be right. In this way, storing something improperly can be a great way to lose it, because the real question here isn't whether you remember their name—I mean, of course you do; it's in your head somewhere—but whether you can recall it when you need to.

In this mode of thinking, asking Greg his age is a good start. Is he forty? Great. He is also a lawyer from Dallas. He has a wife. He's got two kids. He owns a house, and he drives a Toyota. Now, suddenly, Greg isn't just nondescript; he is fleshed out. You only need the name "Greg" to pop out when you meet him, but now he's suddenly Greg the lawyer with two kids. He gets tagged as a father, as a middle-aged man, as a husband, as a lawyer—all these are details your brain can attribute to Greg. His file becomes fuller, more pronounced. As such, it is easier to distinguish from the other files, which are just names. Your brain will put this information together and store it like that. So, if you are talking to someone later on and they ask, "Did you meet Greg? I think you two would get along great!" you may say, "Oh, was he the lawyer from Dallas? Yeah, good guy."

Your brain has an uncanny way of recalling information that is clustered together like this. Song lyrics are a great example. If someone sings a song, you will probably remember the chorus, who wrote it, and possibly even the year it was published. You need to work with your brain when it comes to memory. Understanding how memory works with the development of neural pathways is key to building a better memory. Fleshing out the new information and creating a larger destination for this pathway helps it to sink in faster. When more information travels along the pathway, the pathway will be more likely to become a permanent fixture.

This trick also has an added benefit— it makes it seem like you care about the person you are meeting. We know from business meetings and networking events that learning someone's name and immediately talking about ourselves is a great way to forget names. That's one reason people do forget. They are thinking about what they are going to say next; they are not focusing on the person they are speaking to. You can easily combine this trick with repetition to arm yourself with possibly the best combination tool for remembering names. Introduce yourself first—that is key. Say, "Hi, my name is…" and get them to give you their name. (We'll use "Greg" for this example.)

Your next line is, "Greg, it's great to meet you. So, Greg, what do you do?" You get their name three times in succession and launch into a conversation in which they are giving you details about themselves. You get to appear attentive, and they get to talk about themselves. You also get to hear their name repeated, which, combined with the information you are learning about them, will definitely help you keep them in mind. I can't stress enough the importance of listening to and focusing on the person's words. If you genuinely do not care about them, no tip or trick in the world will help you remember their name.

CHAPTER 5:

MNEMONICS AND OTHER DEVICES

Rhyme and rhythm your way to perfect recall

Mnemonics may be a term you have heard but know little about. It is one of those words that encompasses several different concepts. When we talk about mnemonics, we usually mean an auditory trick to aid memory. However, mnemonics can apply to many things and is roughly defined as the use of pattern to assist with memory. The patterns may be in the form of tones, letters, numbers, shapes, rhymes, or any number of different things. I'll list some of the most common mnemonics to illustrate how simple and common they can be, but also how handy they are for remembering complex things that you'd have no chance at remembering otherwise.

If I had said to four-year-old you, "Memorize this series

of twenty-six numbers," would you have been able to? No? Of course not. You couldn't now. But, strangely, children can master the alphabet with relative ease at the same time they're learning the letters. How? With the aid of a mnemonic device, a song. A-B-C-D, E-F-G, H-I-J-K-L-M-N-O-P, Q-R-S, T-U-V, W, X, Y, and Z. I remember that from when I was four years old, singing it at school. This simple device lets children learn something highly complex, and it gives them the ability to store that information forever. The song makes use of a rhythmic and rhyming mnemonic, adding a melody to information to help it stick.

As illustrated with the alphabet song, rhyme and rhythm has been proven effective throughout history. In fact, using rhyme to commit information to memory is an old tradition. Traditional stories and wisdom were often passed from generation to generation via oral tales, or ballads. Dr. David Rubin's book, "Memory in Oral Traditions," demonstrated that ballads with rhyming words were more easily remembered by college students than non-rhyming ballads. Rhyming makes it easier for the brain to retain information by assigning meaning and sorting those memories into long-term storage.

Another slightly different example is the number of days in each month. You probably remember that one too.

Thirty days hath September, April, June, and dull November. All the rest have thirty-one, except February alone, which has twenty-eight days clear, and twenty-nine on a leap year. Now, once again, this takes a lot of information and makes it not only processable but memorable too. When considering that most people can only recall a string of seven random numbers before they lose track, remembering how many days are in each month is pretty impressive, right? This makes use of a rhyming mnemonic too. While the rhyme differs only slightly from the alphabet song, it showcases how, using pre-existing knowledge, it's possible to insert information other than that which you're trying to learn: the extra words between the months as well as the information that's left out purposefully (the months with thirty-one days).

Another mnemonic device we will cover in this chapter is the use of acronyms. Acronyms can be used in one of two ways. The first is as a straight acronym, like "ROY-G-BIV," to help you remember the colors in the visible light spectrum: red, orange, yellow, green, blue, indigo, violet. The second is as a substituted acronym, like "Richard of York Gave Battle in In Vain," for the light spectrum again, or "Many Vile Earthlings Munch Jam Sandwiches Under Newspaper Piles" for the planets. You can get rid of "piles" if you do not include Pluto in your list of planets and add an "s" to "newspaper" instead. Acronyms appear everywhere in common usage, perhaps without you even knowing. With something like "CIA," which we pronounce "see-eye-ay," it's obvious that it is an acronym. With something like "SWAT" though, which we pronounce as a word and not a series of letters, it can be less obvious. That, in fact, stands for "Special Weapons and Tactics." But we can go one step further, as in "TV" for "television." "TV" is accepted as a word itself and not as a representative of the word it once stood for. Or even—and this is my favorite—"laser." Now, "laser" is special. Once "LASER" (Light Amplification by Stimulated Emission of Radiation), the word is so widely used that it has become a word on its own that doesn't even need capitalization. This is because, much like "TV" and "SWAT," it has gone through what is known as a word formation process. Within that process, the word has undergone clipping, which is a shortening of an existing phrase or word to make it easier for us to say and use. Some other examples include "gasoline" being shortened to "gas," "advertisements" to "ads," and all acronyms. Now, while that's a superbly interesting tangent, can this process of creating acronyms help you remember someone's name? Well, probably—under the right circumstances.

So, let's explore how mnemonics can help you remember someone's name. To fully come to grips with the reason that rhythmic devices and the like make remembering names such a simple process, we need to understand the natural lyricality of words themselves. To do so, we will go through some poetry theory, but don't worry, it will be quick and (relatively) painless.

Rhyme, Meter and, Rhythm

Some people may think poetry is sullen people sitting in a dark room with candles, yelling "woe is me." While this is the case for the opening scene in the 1996 movie version of *Romeo and Juliet*, with Leonardo DiCaprio doing just that—pining after a lost love, poetry is actually very technical, at least for those who are creating what's known as form poetry (poetry with a set structure, not simply writing without rules). With form poetry, a writer must adhere to meter and rhyme. The term rhyme is self-explanatory, obviously, and usually pertains to words that appear at the end of the lines and share a significant sound. Remember "Mike" and "bike" from Chapter 2? That is a full rhyme. In addition to that, you may also be able to utilize something like "Steve" and "stove," which is a half rhyme. That's a sweeping simplification, but I'm sure you know what a rhyme is.

Now, meter is a little different. It's the overarching term

that applies to the number of syllables and the order of the stresses in a line. Words have natural stresses in them. In these words, the bold syllable would be naturally stressed. Blender: Blen-der. Rolling: Roll-ing. Stupid: Stu-pid. Differentiate. Diff-er-en-ti-ate. Electrify. El-ec-tri-fy. Meter refers to the number of words in a line and how the stresses are ordered. By structuring a line with the stresses alternating on and off, we create a rhythm or a beat. Dum-dee, dum-dee, dum-dee…

Why am I going through this? Well, the alphabet song has four stressed syllables in each line, with each stressed syllable followed by an unstressed syllable or a breath. Each line is four trochaic feet, with the song being written in trochaic tetrameter (if you want to get technical), which is the meter. This creates a dum-dee rhythm of stressed and unstressed syllables, giving us a beat. After the seventh syllable, we take a breath, which is our eighth count, and we start the next line. In the example below, unstressed syllables are represented by a hyphen (-) and stressed syllables are represented by a slash (/). Depending on your accent, speech pattern, etc., you may have learned this with the inverse syllables being stressed.

1	+	2	+	3	+	4	+	5	+	6	+	7
/	-	/	-	/	-	/						
A		B		C		D		E		F		G
/	-	/	-	/	-	/						
H		I		J		K		L		MNO		P
/	-	/	-	/	-	/						
Q		R		S		(breath)	T		U			V
/	-	/	-	/	-	/						
Doub-le-U		X		(breath)	Y			and				Z

Following this strict meter creates a beat where there wasn't one before. By using basic poetry theory, we turn twenty-six characters with no discerning features or order into an easy-to-remember song. This sounds like a tall order for remembering someone's name, but have you ever noticed how radio jingles stick in your mind? It's exactly that simple.

/   -   /   -   -   /   -
Greg the law- yer from Dal- las

If you emphasize "Greg," "law-," and "Dal," you create a series of beats. Simply elevate your tone and emphasis on those words to create this down and up rhythm. Using basic techniques like this, advertising companies charge excessive amounts of money to create company jingles and slogans. However, you can exploit this catchy tune to help you remember who Greg is; just don't sing it to him. You can always add more information too, and when it gets too much to create your name jingle, you can transition into acronyms or acronym replacement.

Acronyms

We covered acronyms as to how they are used in learning, and we listed common ones that we utilize every day to help us remember the names of things—remember laser?

Below, I'll show you how you can take the information you learn and organize it into an acronym that may well help you remember not only the person's name, but extra information about them too. Here's a fictional person and some information about them:

Name: Simon Matthews
Occupation: Dentist
Name of Company: Pearls
Company Location: Warrington
Marriage Status: Single
Hometown: Huddersfield

Now, once you've gotten good at remembering names, you can use acronyms to condense all that other information into a manageable lump.

Our letters (excluding Simon) are: M, D, P, W, S, H

One way to use these letters is to assign them a series of words that fit together and precede it with "Simon" (e.g., Simon Makes Delightful Pies with Savory Ham).

Or, you can attempt to make a word out of those letters. S, M, D, P, W, S, H. You may notice a distinct lack of vowels, which makes word formation difficult. Maybe it doesn't matter where he is from or what his marital status is. What you may need to know is his name, occupation, the name of his company, and where it is based. S, M, D, P, W. Adding in vowels could give you SAMPAW or SMODPOW. You can then attribute that to him, with his first name either omitted or included: Simon AMPAW, Simon MODPOW, SAMPAW, or SMODPOW. Now, while you only have to remember one word, you are actually memorizing a set of information. Acronyms, like the image triggers we covered in Chapter 2, rely on the brain being able to make connections from pre-existing information. By remembering the acronym, you are much more likely to remember what it stands for, and you only need to keep track of one word, not five.

While this may be a slight overcomplication, I wanted to illustrate how these types of acronyms can work. While this probably isn't as effective or efficient as the jingle method, if you need to memorize long strings of information that are, shall we say…dry, it may be helpful to get into the habit of developing acronyms and replacements like these.

Alliteration

The last and final thing I'd like to mention before we move on is the simple use of alliteration. You may recall classic tongue twisters such as, "Sally sells sea shells by the seashore" or "Peter Piper picked a peck of pickled peppers." The alliteration is part of what made these tongue twisters challenging to say, and they are funny, so our brain naturally remembers. You can also employ assonance (repeating vowel sounds) or consonance (repeating consonant sounds) to aid with rhythmic memory, but alliteration is the best place to start. However, this may only apply to certain situations. When we talk about using rhyme, it doesn't need to be complex, and it can be as simple as: "David the accountant likes money because he can count it." If one comes into your head, use it. Using alliteration with "Greg" and "lawyer" and "Dallas" might prove tricky, but when it comes to David, it might roll off the tongue: "Dodgy David does dastardly dealings for his accountancy firm." It may not be true, and it may not be perfect, but simply using a word that begins with the same letter as a name or rhymes with the name can be super effective. "Funny Fred," "Smart Sarah," or even something like "Overweight Oliver" might help you. It may not be appropriate, and it may be a little mean, but it is only in your head, and nobody will judge you.

As I've said before, none of these is foolproof, but using a combination of all of them, in the right situations, means you will always have a tool that's perfect for remembering someone's name at your disposal.

CHAPTER 6:

THE MEMORY PALACE

Infinite rooms, infinite doors, infinite memory

The "memory palace" memory technique is one of those things that doesn't quite seem real and, for many people, will always remain an impossibility because of the sheer scale of it. It is a technique that was used long ago by the Ancient Greeks. It was allegedly introduced to the Romans by the Greek poet, Simonides, who was credited with developing the technique. The trick with the memory palace is to use it for everything, and once you start, you can never stop. However, if you can master it, you can become one of those formidable people who remember everything.

What does it entail? Basically, it is taking a very strong image that you have of a place—the house you lived in as a kid, your home now, your office, your school—anywhere that you can picture clearly enough to walk around in your mind. It needs to be somewhere you know so well that you can walk through it in darkness. If you cannot think of a building you know well enough, use a room and the furniture in it as your memory palace.

In that memory palace, you must be able to pick out individual locations (sometimes referred to as a "locus"), each of which must be utterly clear in your mind. While entering your childhood home's memory palace, the first locus may be the welcome mat, the shoe rack, or the coat hooks. If you use only one room (e.g., living room), you may use the furniture or other fixtures as your locus points. The trick with this list is that they are already very clear in your mind. It is also strongly recommended that you form a linear path around each room, or from room to room. When trying to memorize lists or items, like a shopping list or a phone number, you take each individual item and place it in a locus, creating and exaggerating a visual image for effect. The linear path is important to help embed the items in your memory and recall the information later.

So, a shopping list may include carrots, milk, and onions. As you open your memory palace door, you see a giant onion sitting on your welcome mat. He looks up at you and says in an over-the-top Brooklyn accent, "Hey, I'm sitting here!" Then you turn to see a living carrot sticking out of your father's boots, and she asks, "Does this fake tan make me look orange?" After that, you turn to the coat hooks, where a bottle of milk is sulking. You ask what's wrong, and the onion tells you not to bother with him, as "he's been sour ever since he missed his date."

This seems stupid—absurd, even—and utterly idiotic, but for people with strong visual memories, this hyperbolic scenario can be a wonderful way to help people remember long sets of information. Humor is a great device too, and aids in this method. Some people have a real proclivity for remembering humorous things—like those people who remember really long jokes. By having these items all alive, full of character, and placed in familiar locations, as well as interacting with them in a specific order, you can build your memory palace and walk through it as many times as you like. Keep your visual path the same as your real path through that palace, and you may be one of the people who can place things in there and never lose them.

As your house begins to fill, your brain will become used to it. You can slowly start to create a much larger palace in your head. Behind each door in your palace is a location you know well, accessible through a central corridor. People who apply this method spend years practicing it. It is helpful for people who practice the art of mentalism; to be good at that, you need near-perfect recall. This method was popularized by the TV show, *The Mentalist*; however, a lot of real guides exist and go into far greater detail than we have. For remembering names, the idea would be to meet someone and have them sit at the dinner table in your memory palace. Imagining them in familiar surroundings could be the trick to never forget a face or a name again.

This is also a great way, if you are finding it easy to build your memory palace, to remember multiple names. We used the example of the dinner party in Chapter 2 when we went over mnemonic triggers. It is always a great image to work with inside the memory palace because most of us have a very clear image of our dinner tables from our childhood or current homes. We can picture them empty or full, with as many or as few people as we like. When you enter a party or gathering with lots of people and meet someone, simply seat them at your dinner table. When they tell you their name, write it on a sign, and hang it around their neck. You are now utilizing the spell-it-out technique we covered above, and if you write "Tall Alex" instead of "Alex," you are also putting into practice the random-trigger technique we covered earlier. Again, have them do something outrageous to embed the idea (e.g. have Tall Alex bang his head on the ceiling because he's so tall). Combining these three techniques can be a great way to remember multiple names, and once they are inside your palace… Well, you know that the doors only open for you.

This strategy isn't just a great way to remember names. A good number of contestants who win memory contests use this technique to help them recall numbers and lists of words. Some stage magicians also use a variation of the memory palace technique to perform card tricks. Researchers have performed studies on memory contest champions to understand how their brains function when they walk through their palaces. It was discovered that the success of memory champions is not dependent on the persons' intelligence, nor do they have brains that are structured differently from anyone else. What they do have is excellent spatial memory. All of us use spatial memory to help us find our way around town, and it is what laboratory rats use to navigate through a maze to look for food.

CHAPTER 7:

FICTIONALIZATION

You're not real—at least not in my head

This is another slightly specialized technique that may not be effective for everyone, but for those with an active imagination, it may be a very handy way to keep track of people's identities. The human brain has a natural preference for stories, which means linking names you want to remember to a story or fictional world makes the names stick better.

The idea here is to have a narrative world in your head—something differentiated from reality enough to be distinct, but with a framework that lies over the top. A fantasy realm is great, but don't go too crazy, as you have to be able to relate your information to reality. A sci-fi world is also perfect, as is a sixties-set, Cold-War spy theme.

So, what's the trick? Well, in the real world, you might be

a real estate agent—not hugely exciting. In your fantasy world, you work as the king's royal envoy, and your job is to place warriors and noble families in their perfect castles to aid the kingdom in its conquests.

So, in your mind, you're not meeting Mr. and Mrs. Johnson at the three-bedroom detached on Millbrook Avenue—you're meeting Sir and Lady Johnson, who are fresh from the Battle of the Three Dragons, where he slew a mighty beast with his broadsword. When you meet him, you discover that he's bald. That's not a fashion choice. No, he lost his hair as he rode his stallion straight down the throat of the dragon. Its fire burned off all of his hair. And that scar on his wife's face? That's not from falling off her bike as a child. No, an assassin broke into her bedchamber at night to take revenge for the killing of his queen. He almost got her, but she sleeps with a stiletto under her pillow for this very reason.

Now, that's some interesting stuff, right? Chances are no one will ever ask you why he's bald or why she's got a scar, so those amazing stories only live in your head and make the people you're meeting more interesting.

If you think the spy thriller may be more exciting, perhaps Eleanor the actuary is a Russian spy out to infiltrate the government. I mean, come on, no one can be that boring without using it as a cover, can they? Or, if you are into superheroes, ocean, or outer space, perhaps you could use that as your fictional world. By attributing these fantastical things to people, you turn them into living, breathing action heroes and heroines. They become utterly memorable, and by that very fact, live in your mind as a mix of fantasy and reality—Mr. Johnson the school teacher on the outside, and a dragonfire-singed, battle-hardened monster slayer on the inside.

Again, it may only work from time to time, and it is one

of those methods that once you start, you can't really stop. But this is a really handy way to keep track of people and help them stick in your mind. Remember not to bow to pseudo-strangers and call them "sire" or "lord." That can get embarrassing.

CONCLUSION

The Science Behind It

Understanding how our brain works is another important key to improving memory and recall. The more you understand how memories are made and processed, the better you will be able to apply the techniques covered in this book.

Memory processing takes place in different areas throughout the brain. Memories and the ability to recall them consist of several different systems, each with their own part to play when it comes to collecting, storing, and recalling information.

Sensory data: It all begins with your senses, which are continually collecting information every second of each day. With so much information being collected through your senses, it would be nearly impossible for all of it to be processed and stored. Therefore, parts of your brain, specifically the hippocampus and the frontal cortex, work together to sort everything as it comes into your brain. Scientists are still working to figure out how exactly this sorting occurs, but they do know all sensory data is identified and discarded or stored in the brain.

Encoding: This is the first step in the memory process and it begins with paying attention. To help your brain properly encode something, you must focus and give it your attention. Many of the tricks covered in this book, such as repetition, are ways to signal your brain to pay attention to something you want to remember.

Encoding involves four categories:

- what we hear (acoustic)
- what we touch (tactile)
- what we see (visual)
- the interpretation of the meaning of words (semantics)

When it comes to remembering names, you must pay attention and focus so you hear the name during the encoding process. If you are distracted, thinking about how you are going to respond, chances are the name won't be properly encoded, and it will impact your ability to recall that information.

There are three storage systems involved with memory,

which is primarily a right-brain function. These storage sections are found throughout the brain's network, and each one plays a different role in making memories.

Short-Term Memory: Many experts agree that this is the storage area where data ends up first if it isn't immediately discarded. When it comes to short-term memory, acoustic encoding (what we hear) is primary. This area has a limited amount of storage capacity. For most people, this means five to seven items at a time for less than thirty seconds. You may extend this capacity slightly by repeating a name several times within those initial seconds, visualizing yourself spelling it out (to engage more than one segment of the brain), and linking it to an image or another meaningful existing memory. Memories that are encoded properly can make their way into long-term memory.

Long-Term Memory: This is the storage space for memories that our brain deems important and is primarily reliant on semantic encoding. Semantic memory storage is where all your school-related memory, song lyrics, and other memorable information are stored. Some long-term memory can be episodic. These are the memories tied to meaningful personal events—the ones that are full of emotions. This is the reason that song lyrics or other memorable things, which are tied to important or emotional events, will be sorted more easily into your long-term memory.

Recall Memory: Your brain uses recall memory to seek information previously stored within your brain. If you are someone who tends to forget names, one reason could be that you aren't giving them enough attention to allow them to be properly encoded in the first place. You can't recall what isn't there.

The ability to recall information is also higher with visual images and with images or stories that are unusual or unexpected. It's also easier to recall groups of information than a single piece. Recall is a complex process; a simpler way to think about recall is to imagine you were looking for a needle in a haystack versus a package of needles or several spools of thread. The more associations you can encode with the information the first time, the deeper the neural pathway will be built within your brain's network. You essentially turn one lone needle into something larger and easier to find.

Memory palace and fictionalization work better when you visualize them, group them, tie them to a story, and make them outlandish. Using these tricks to associate a name strengthens the pathway to that information. It is a bit like tying that lone needle to several different threads that when pulled will bring the needle into view. When it comes time to remember information, such as a name, the recall time is correlated to how strong the associations or neural pathway was for that name.

A Quick Recap

Well, there you have it. Our top seven techniques for memorizing the names of everyone you meet, as well as some bonus tips on memory in general. You'll surely want to try them all, and that's the right thing to do. Keep practicing, and no doubt, some will jump out at you as more effective than others. Everyone's mind is different, so what works for your buddy may not work for you. I, for one, have the most luck with the fictionalization and information-grouping methods, but I have a very active imagination, and everyone appears to me as a battle-hardened space outlaw from a mixed-up galaxy under the rule of an evil overlord. But you know—to each their own.

Start at the beginning and work your way through. Remember: *paying attention is the key to proper encoding.* In fact, you may see significant improvement in your ability to remember names simply by paying attention when you first meet someone. Get into the habit of repetition. You may find that once you practice, it will become the only tool you ever need. However, you may find that spelling it on a chalkboard will do the trick, or if you watch a lot of TV, perhaps image linking to an existing memory will be your best bet. Perhaps you're a musician who will really get into mnemonics. Who can say? What we do know is that each of these is tried, tested, and effective in its own right; you have to focus, concentrate, and practice.

Made in the USA
Monee, IL
29 November 2019

17586684R10036